Puffin Books

The Animal Quiz Book

Why do crocodiles swallow stones? Which bird migrates the furthest? Can kangaroos swim?

With over a million species, the animal kingdom provides a limitless source of fascinating questions. It is a colourful, incredible world, full of ingenuity and full of surprises.

Sally Kilroy has assembled a feast for enquiring minds; from Domestic Animals to Dinosaurs, Fish to Footprints and Reptiles to Record Breakers. Discover where creatures live, how they adapt to their conditions, the way they treat each other, the dangers they face – you will be amazed at how much you *didn't* know!

The Animal Quiz Book opens up the astonishing world which surrounds us. Fact-finding can be fun, so have a go! Delve in, bombard your brain and gamble on a guess before sneaking a look at the answers!

D0494724

Sally Kilroy

The Animal Quiz Book

Puffin Books

Puffin Books, Penguin Books Ltd, Harmondsworth, Middlesex, England
Viking Penguin Inc., 40 West 23rd Street, New York, New York 10010, U.S.A.
Penguin Books Australia Ltd, Ringwood, Victoria, Australia
Penguin Books Canada Ltd, 2801 John Street, Markham, Ontario, Canada L3R 1B4
Penguin Books (N.Z.) Ltd, 182–190 Wairau Road, Auckland 10, New Zealand

First published 1985

Made and printed in Great Britain by
Cox & Wyman Ltd, Reading
Typeset in 10/12 pt Linotron Univers Light by
Rowland Phototypesetting Ltd, Bury St Edmunds, Suffolk

For Ben and Nick

Contents

THE QUESTIONS

Animal Homes

Some animals, like fish, have no proper home; others find a ready-made shelter like a crevice amongst rocks. Many animals, however, take great time and trouble to build their homes. They usually guard their homes or the area in which they live.

1 What is an eagle's nest called?

2 What is a group of rabbits' homes called?

3 Whose nest is called a drey?
   (a) A hedgehog
   (b) A harvest mouse
   (c) A squirrel

4 What is an otter's home called?
   (a) A lodge
   (b) A dam
   (c) A holt

5 Which bird sometimes builds a huge nest on a chimney top?
  (a) The swan
  (b) The pelican
  (c) The stork

6 Which bird from Eastern Asia makes a nest by sewing leaves together with it's beak?
  (a) The weaverbird
  (b) The tailorbird
  (c) The crossbill

7 The kingfisher digs a tunnel in the river bank with a chamber
at the end for its nest. What does it line the nest with?
   (a) Feathers
   (b) Dry fish bones
   (c) Twigs and leaves

8 Which bird nests under the eaves of buildings?
   (a) The house martin
   (b) The swallow
   (c) The swift

9 Which animal lives in a lodge?
   (a) An otter
   (b) A water rat
   (c) A beaver

10 What is a badger's home called?
   (a) An earth
   (b) A burrow
   (c) A set

11 What is the name given to the shelter where a she-wolf has her cubs?
(a) A lair
(b) A den
(c) An earth

12 How high are termite mounds?
(a) Up to 1 metre
(b) Up to 8 metres
(c) Up to 11 metres

13 A lot of animals provide a home for fleas. Which of the following are the most flea-ridden?
(a) Cats
(b) Rabbits
(c) Red squirrels

Fact: A nest built by a pair of bald eagles in America measured 2.59 metres wide and 3.65 metres deep!

Fact: The social weaverbird of South Africa builds a large communal nest with separate compartments for as many as 200 pairs.

Families

Some animals give their young no help, and some even eat them! Others build elaborate nests where they can be raised, and some apes look after their young for years. In several species the male animals do more than the females to look after the babies.

1 How many eggs does a puffin usually lay?
  (a) 7
  (b) 1
  (c) 3

2 What do frogs' eggs hatch into?

3 Which of these snakes lay eggs?: boas or pythons?

4 What are baby sheep called?

5 What is a leveret?
  (a) A baby swan
  (b) A baby otter
  (c) A baby hare

6 Baby bears are very small at first. How do they keep warm?
  (a) By lying in the sun
  (b) By hugging their mother
  (c) By going for a run

7 Can you name the two mammals which lay eggs?

8 What are young fish called?

9 What is a baby kangaroo called
  when it is in its mother's pouch?

10 A baby kangaroo moves out of its mother's pouch when it is too big; at what age does this happen?
(a) 8 weeks
(b) 6 months
(c) 2 years

11 Do baby moles have any fur when they are born?

12 How long do dragonfly babies (nymphs) live and grow in the water after hatching?
(a) 3 days
(b) 6 weeks
(c) 2–3 years

13 What is a young lion called?

14 Which mammal carries its baby inside it longest before it is born?
(a) The giant panda
(b) The white rhinoceros
(c) The Asiatic elephant

15 Which fish makes a nest of bubbles to put its eggs in until they hatch?
(a) The trout
(b) The minnow
(c) The fighting fish

16 Which bird lays its eggs in another bird's nest?

17 Where do baby scorpions live until they can fend for themselves?
 (a) In a burrow
 (b) In a rock crevice
 (c) On their mothers' backs

18 Do frogs' eggs have shells?

19 Which one of the following does not carry its baby in a pouch: wombat, koala, opossum, panda, bandicoot?

20 What are baby squirrels called?

21 How many lots of babies do most types of squirrel have each year?

22 Do all birds hatch from eggs?

23 Why does a female bird sit on her eggs?

24 For how long do young chimpanzees stay with their mothers?
 (a) About four weeks
 (b) About ten months
 (c) About six years

25 After they are laid, seahorse eggs are carried in a pouch on the adult's belly until they hatch. Which parent carries them?

26 What is a baby horse called?

27 Which baby animals like piggyback rides?
   (a) Koalas
   (b) Kangaroos
   (c) Spiny anteaters

28 Which bird lays the biggest egg in relation to its own size?
   (a) The ostrich
   (b) The kiwi
   (c) The pelican

29 What does a female bat generally do with her young when she searches for food?
   (a) She leaves them under a pile of stones
   (b) She pushes them into a crack in the cave
   (c) She leaves them hanging up

30 Sea turtles lay eggs in pits on sandy shores. What do the babies do when they hatch?
   (a) Call out for food
   (b) Scurry into the sea
   (c) Huddle in groups to keep warm

Fact: Tree shrews build a separate nest for their babies. The mother visits the nursery only every one or two days, but the babies can drink a great deal at a time.

Fact: Baby kangaroos have exciting rides in their mother's pouch as she can leap 7 metres in one jump.

Living Together

Some animals like to be on their own. Others move about in groups. Leaders are chosen by fighting. In the breeding season, males go to great lengths to attract females.

1 What is a group of chimpanzees called?
   (a) A herd
   (b) A colony
   (c) A troop

2 What is the name given to a male kangaroo?

3 Which male animal is called a Tom?

4 What is a group of lions called?

5 What is this frog doing?
   (a) It is going to have babies
   (b) It is calling out to attract a female and warn off other males
   (c) It is storing food to digest later

6 What is a small group of goldfinches called?
   (a) A drove
   (b) A charm
   (c) A flock

7 How does a male gorilla keep order when the females in his group squabble?
   (a) He chases one away
   (b) He throws leaves at them
   (c) He stares fiercely at them

8 What do we call a group of porpoises?
   (a) A shoal
   (b) A colony
   (c) A school

9 Do adult giant pandas live alone, in pairs or in groups?

10 What are male and female salmon called?

11 Which male bird has a tail that he can spread into a beautiful fan of plumes?

12 Which young fish is called a Jack?
    (a) A young trout
    (b) A young pike
    (c) A young carp

13 Which of these females is called a Jill?
    (a) A badger
    (b) A polecat
    (c) A dog

14 Which bird makes a mound 15 centimetres high and 90 centimetres across to dance on in order to attract females?
    (a) The jungle babbler
    (b) The superb lyrebird
    (c) The northern mocking bird

15 How do chimpanzees establish themselves as leaders?
 (a) By fighting
 (b) By throwing a tantrum
 (c) By beating their chests

16 What is a hob?
 (a) A male ferret
 (b) A male stoat
 (c) A male weasel

17 The male is called a billy, the female a nanny and the young a kid. Which animal is it?

18 Why do some male newts go bright colours and grow bigger fins?
 (a) To scare off enemies
 (b) To attract females
 (c) To be hidden among the bright plants where they live

19 Which of these females is sometimes called a queen?
 (a) A pig
 (b) A cat
 (c) A gerbil

20 Which bird imprisons his mate in the nest?
  (a) The toucan
  (b) The woodpecker
  (c) The hornbill

21 What is a female donkey sometimes called?

22 Which ducks 'quack', males or females?

23 Whalebone whales eat krill, small shrimp-like animals. What is the correct name for a large group of krill?
  (a) A shoal
  (b) A swarm
  (c) A herd

24 The male midwife toad carries the eggs around after they are laid until they are ready to hatch into tadpoles. How does he carry them?
(a) Wrapped round his back legs
(b) In a pouch on his tummy
(c) In his mouth

25 Which bull and cow have a young pup?
(a) Cattle
(b) Dogs
(c) Seals

26 What is a male pig called?

27 Guillemots take it in turns to look after their egg, holding it between their feet and body. Why is the egg pear-shaped?
(a) Because the baby has a big head
(b) Because it is squeezed out of shape as it is laid
(c) So it doesn't roll away when the parents change places

28 What is a female fox called?

Fact: Satin and regent bowerbirds paint the inside of the bower (nest) with blue or green pigments mixed with saliva. They use a leaf or piece of bark as a brush.

Animal Bodies

Animals are specially equipped for the way in which they live. Birds have feathers so they can fly. Other animals have ways of keeping warm or keeping cool. Even their feet differ to suit the surfaces that they live on.

1 What is the term for animals with backbones?

2 Do birds have backbones?

3 What do we call all the bones that form the framework of a body?

4 Which animal has a horn on its nose?

5 In what way is a toad's tongue different from a human's?

6 Which rodent is covered in quills?

7 How many tentacles does an octopus have?

8 Which group of animals grows hair and has females who produce milk to feed their young?
(a) Mammals
(b) Reptiles
(c) Birds

9 Do seals have feet?

10 After man, elephants are the longest living mammals; how long do they live?
(a) 30–40 years
(b) 45–55 years
(c) 60–70 years

11 Apart from its tusks, how many teeth does an elephant have?
(a) 4
(b) 14
(c) 28

12 Why do camels have long eyelashes?

13 Do any snakes have feet?

14 Which animal grows the largest horns?
(a) The waterbuck
(b) The Texas longhorn steer
(c) The Indian buffalo

15 Which mammal that lives on land has the most keenly developed sense of hearing?
(a) The rabbit
(b) The roe deer
(c) The bat

16 Snakes never blink because they have no eyelids. What do we call the glassy scale that covers each eye?
(a) A transparent lid
(b) A lens
(c) A spectacle

17 Most mammals have seven neck-bones. How many does a giraffe have?
(a) 13
(b) 7
(c) 28

18 Do all centipedes have 100 legs?

19 Do turtles have teeth?

20 Unlike many insects, a grasshopper has ears. Where are they?

21 How thick is an elephant's skin?
   (a) Less than 2 millimetres
   (b) At least 7 millimetres
   (c) At least 12 millimetres

22 Have horses always had hoofs?

23 One reptile can move its eyes individually, catch insects with a tongue almost as long as its body and change colour to match its surroundings. What is it?
   (a) A gecko
   (b) An iguana
   (c) A chameleon

Fact: A bird's light weight helps it to fly. Many of its bones are hollow and it has a small number of large air-sacs throughout its body. The body itself is very streamlined.

Fact: A large bird of prey can see more sharply than a human. It is thought that in clear conditions a golden eagle can see a hare 3.2 kilometres away.

Domestic Animals

The first animals to be tamed and live with human beings were dogs. Stone Age man hunted with them. Since then, animals have been used to produce milk, meat and clothing as well as for transport and hauling implements or loads. Many animals are also kept as pets.

1 What breed of dog is used to pull sleighs in the Arctic?
   (a) The labrador
   (b) The dalmatian
   (c) The husky

2 Which is the least intelligent domestic bird?
   (a) The chicken
   (b) The turkey
   (c) The duck

3 Which of these cats has long fur?
(a) The Persian
(b) The Manx
(c) The Siamese

4 Which is the smallest of these ponies?
(a) The Exmoor
(b) The Shetland
(c) The New Forest

5 What sort of animals are called Plymouth Rock, Rhode Island Red and Buff Orpington?

6 What colour eyes do white rabbits often have?

7 Are puppies and kittens born with their eyes open or shut?

8 Millions of golden hamsters are kept as pets. Where do they come from?
(a) Syria
(b) Cornwall
(c) Finland

9 What is the name given to the coat of a sheep?

10 Which dogs are used for mountain rescue work in the Alps?
   (a) Alsatians
   (b) Labradors
   (c) St Bernards

11 What is the commonest ailment in horses?
   (a) Colic (tummy-ache)
   (b) A cough
   (c) A cold

12 The chihuahua is the smallest breed of dog. Which country did it first come from?
   (a) Spain
   (b) Mexico
   (c) China

13 What sort of animal is a Jersey?
  (a) A goat
  (b) A cow
  (c) A sheep

14 Where did goldfish originally come from?
  (a) South Africa
  (b) China and Japan
  (c) Hawaii

15 For how long have horses been domesticated?
  (a) 600 years
  (b) 1,200 years
  (c) 4,000 years

16 Which cats have blue eyes?

17 Which birds are used for racing?

18 What sort of animal is a tabby?

19 What is a pedigree dog?
(a) A South American hunting dog
(b) A high quality dog whose family can be traced
(c) A dog used by the fishermen of Labrador to swim in with nets

20 The Angus, the Friesian and the Ayrshire are breeds of what type of animal?

21 What was the original reason for clipping poodles' coats into patterns?
(a) To make them look pretty
(b) To make them lighter for swimming
(c) To make people laugh in the circus

22 Why do horses usually sleep standing up?
(a) They feel warmer like that
(b) They can breathe better
(c) They can run off quickly if they are frightened

23 Which dog has a blue tongue?
   (a) The chow
   (b) The dachshund
   (c) The boxer

24 How does a shepherd catch a sheep?
   (a) With a rugger-tackle
   (b) By catching its hind leg or neck
   (c) By throwing a net over it

25 What is the largest litter of piglets on record?
   (a) 11
   (b) 17
   (c) 34

26 Border collies are working dogs. What are they used for?
  (a) Chasing foxes
  (b) Moving sheep
  (c) Guarding places at night

27 Which dogs were often kept to run beside coaches and keep off highwaymen?
  (a) Mastiffs
  (b) Great Danes
  (c) Dalmatians

28 How high was the tallest horse ever recorded?
  (a) 17.2 hands (1.78 metres)
  (b) 18.1 hands (1.85 metres)
  (c) 21.1 hands (2.16 metres)

29 Which reptile that lives in a shell is often kept as a pet?

Fact: The most unlikely match in the dog world was when a Great Dane bitch produced thirteen puppies fathered by a dachshund.

Signs and Footprints

You can often see which animals have passed by from the things they have left behind, such as footprints, the remains of food and droppings.

1 Who has been using a tree stump as a dining table and left behind a lot of cracked acorns?
  (a) A mink
  (b) A squirrel
  (c) A pine marten

2 What do we call the paths regularly used by small mammals?
  (a) Tracks
  (b) Runs
  (c) Burrows

3 Who might leave fish remains on the river bank?
   (a) An otter
   (b) A kingfisher
   (c) A water vole

4 Which animal might leave berries hidden in a hollow trunk?
   (a) A vole
   (b) A blackbird
   (c) A wood-mouse

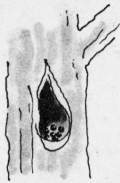

5 Which spiders spin a blanket-like web on a plant and wait below until the surrounding trip wires toss the prey into the web?
   (a) Spitting spiders
   (b) Purseweb spiders
   (c) Money spiders

6 What are deer droppings called?
   (a) Currants
   (b) Crotties
   (c) Spraints

7 Which animal eats honeysuckle bark and leaves?
   (a) The dormouse
   (b) The squirrel
   (c) The water vole

8 Who might have eaten a fungus if parts were gone but there were no teeth marks?
(a) A wood-mouse
(b) A squirrel
(c) A slug

9 Which of these would leave a dead chicken with its head bitten off?
(a) A stoat
(b) A fox
(c) A badger

10 Which of these birds has webbed feet: a mallard, a kingfisher or a heron?

11 These footprints belong to a dog and a cat. Which is which?

(a)   (b)

12 Who would this track belong to: a hedgehog, a house mouse or a squirrel?

13 Is this the footprint of a pig, a sheep or a cow?

14 Who left these tracks: a weasel, a rabbit or a badger?

On the Seashore

Animals from many groups live on sandy or rocky shores. Crustaceans, like shrimps and crabs, belong to the Arthropod group, which includes insects. This is the largest group. Molluscs make up the second-largest group, which includes squids and octopuses and animals like mussels which have a hard shell to protect them. Those with one shell are called univalves, and those with two, bivalves. Sea urchins and starfish come from the Echinoderm (spiny-skinned) group. There are also worms, jellyfish and other animals like birds that feed on the creatures of the seashore.

1 Which of these does not have a tail?
 (a) A shrimp
 (b) A lobster
 (c) A crab

2 Where would you find a limpet?
 (a) Clinging to a rock
 (b) Buried under sand
 (c) Floating in shallow water

3 What is this?

 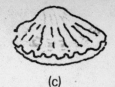

(a)   (b)   (c)

4 Which of these is a bivalve?
  (a) The cowrie
  (b) The whelk
  (c) The cockle

5 Lobsters are red when they are cooked. What colour are they when they are alive?
  (a) Purple
  (b) Blue
  (c) Orange

6 What width could an adult octopus measure with its tentacles stretched out?
  (a) 4.8 metres
  (b) 3.6 metres
  (c) 9.5 metres

7 Which of these might you find clinging to the bottom of a boat?
  (a) A barnacle
  (b) An anemone
  (c) A limpet

8 Is a barnacle a mollusc or a crustacean?

9 How many known species of sea urchin are there?
  (a) 20
  (b) 170
  (c) 800

10 What colour are the beak and legs of the black-headed gull?
  (a) Yellow
  (b) Red
  (c) Blue

11 How many legs does a shrimp have?

12 Which is the largest starfish found around Britain?
  (a) The spiny starfish
  (b) The common starfish
  (c) The cushion starfish

13 Are sponges animals or plants?

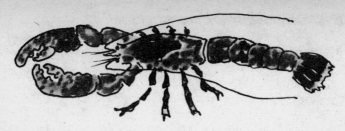

14 Which is the biggest crustacean found in British waters?
    (a) The spider crab
    (b) The edible crab
    (c) The common lobster

15 Where might you find a cockle?
    (a) On rocks
    (b) In the sea
    (c) In sand or sandy mud

16 How can you tell the age of a cockle?

17 If a starfish loses an arm, can it grow a new one?

18 Where you would look for a lobster's eyes?
    (a) On their shells
    (b) On their claws
    (c) On stalks

19 Which are longer, the feelers that prawns and shrimps have, or their bodies?

20 What is a venus flower basket?
   (a) A jellyfish
   (b) A sponge
   (c) A sea anemone

21 How do starfish open an oyster to eat it?
   (a) By smashing it with a pebble
   (b) By pulling it open with their arms
   (c) By squirting poison into the shell

22 Which of these animals is jet-propelled?
   (a) A jellyfish
   (b) A cuttle fish
   (c) A water flea

23 Corals form reefs, especially in tropical waters. They have external skeletons which often form beautiful shapes. What are corals formed by?
   (a) Old shells
   (b) Dead seaweed
   (c) Tiny animals

24 Where does a hermit crab live?
  (a) Attached by suckers to a fish
  (b) In the empty shell of a winkle or whelk
  (c) In a burrow in the sand

25 What does an oyster-catcher eat?
  (a) Mussels
  (b) Seaweed
  (c) Oysters

26 Most jellyfish swim by opening and closing their umbrella. True or false?

Fact: The smallest crabs in the world are pea crabs which are parasites and live in the shells of molluscs like oysters and mussels.

Fact: Shells are built up in three layers – a horny outer one, then a chalky one and a shiny inner one.

Fact: Sea urchins have no head or tail so they can move forward in any direction.

Fact: Most prawns and shrimps can change colour to blend in with their surroundings.

The Record Breakers

Which is the biggest, smallest or fastest of them all?

1 What is the biggest animal that has ever lived?

2 Which is the fastest land animal over a distance of 400 metres?

3 Which is the largest deer in the world?
 (a) The red deer
 (b) The Alaskan moose
 (c) The reindeer

4 Which is the largest bird now in existence?

5 How big is the largest recorded frog?
(a) 26.5 centimetres
(b) 37 centimetres
(c) 81.5 centimetres

6 What is the longest an elephant has been known to live?
(a) 23 years
(b) 70 years
(c) 114 years

7 The longest tusks ever found belonged to a prehistoric elephant. How long were they?
(a) 1.5 metres
(b) 5 metres
(c) 6.5 metres

8 The greatest mouser on record was a cat called Mickey, owned by a Lancashire firm. In his 23 years with them, how many mice did he kill?
(a) Over 17,000
(b) Over 22,000
(c) Over 31,000

9 Which is the fastest wild animal in the British Isles?

10 Which is the largest native British butterfly?
(a) The painted lady
(b) The swallowtail
(c) The brimstone

11 Which is the tallest living animal?

12 Which is Britain's smallest flesh-eating mammal?
  (a) The snipe
  (b) The weasel
  (c) The rabbit

13 The Etruscan shrew is the world's smallest mammal. How much does it weigh?
  (a) 2 grams
  (b) 12 grams
  (c) 22 grams

14 Which is now the largest wild rodent in Britain?

Fact: The heaviest load ever hauled by a pair of draught-horses was 130.6 tonnes – on a special sledge. This is the equivalent of 14½ double-decker buses.

Dinosaurs and Other Prehistoric Animals

These animals lived before writing was invented; the first of them came on to land 400 million years ago. We can learn most about them from their skeletons, some of which have turned into fossils and been preserved in rock. Present-day animals have evolved from these original ones, which died out as other animals developed or as the weather or land changed.

1 What were the first of these to survive on land?
  (a) Fish
  (b) Birds
  (c) Reptiles

2 What were the biggest four-footed animals in history?
  (a) Mammoths
  (b) Dinosaurs
  (c) Elephants

3 The longest dinosaur was Diplodocus (28 metres long). How big was its brain?
  (a) The size of a hen's egg
  (b) The size of an orange
  (c) The size of a football

4 What does the word dinosaur mean?

5 Did dinosaurs eat meat or plants?

6 The biggest dinosaur with horns was about 8 metres long. What is its name?

7 What does the name brontosaurus mean?

8 About how many tonnes did a brontosaurus weigh?
   (a) 35 tonnes
   (b) 70 tonnes
   (c) 115 tonnes

9 Which dinosaur had large bony plates along its back and spikes on its tail?
   (a) Brachiosaurus
   (b) Triceratops
   (c) Stegosaurus

10 Diplodocus was the longest animal ever to walk on land. How long was it?
   (a) As long as one bus
   (b) As long as three buses
   (c) As long as five buses

11 What was the name of the biggest flesh-eating animal ever?

12 What does the name stegosaurus mean?
    (a) Bony lizard
    (b) Roof lizard
    (c) Storm lizard

13 About how long ago did dinosaurs disappear?
    (a) 100 million years ago
    (b) 60 million years ago
    (c) 10 million years ago

14 Why did dinosaurs die out?
    (a) Some new amphibians came and ate them all
    (b) The climate got colder and they couldn't keep warm
    (c) They were wiped out by disease

15 What is a fossil?
   (a) A tiger moth caterpillar
   (b) A freshwater barnacle
   (c) Traces of an organism preserved in rock

16 What is a fossil made of ?
   (a) Clay
   (b) Stone
   (c) Chalk

17 Did dinosaurs lay eggs?

18 Some pelycosaurs before dinosaurs had sails on their backs.
   What do scientists think they were for?
   (a) To pick up sounds
   (b) To stop predators jumping on their backs
   (c) To keep warm

19 How long ago did prehistoric whales (basilosaurus) live?
   (a) 70,000 years ago
   (b) 40 million years ago
   (c) 100 million years ago

20 What sort of animal was a woolly mammoth?
   (a) A reindeer
   (b) A bison
   (c) An elephant

21 About the time of the Ice Age, something bubbled up from the ground and formed pools which animals got trapped in. What was it?
(a) Mud
(b) Tar
(c) Quicksand

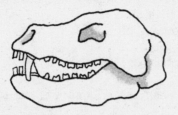

22 If you found a skull with three different sorts of teeth, would it be a reptile's or a mammal's?

23 Mammoths' bodies have been found in Siberia, Russia. How had they been preserved?
(a) Under water
(b) In ice
(c) In mud

24 In one country, all the prehistoric mammals were marsupials – that is, they had pouches. Which country was it?
- (a) Africa
- (b) Australia
- (c) Russia

25 What do we call a person who studies fossils to find out about prehistoric life?
- (a) A palaeontologist
- (b) An ornithologist
- (c) A meteorologist

Fact: One dinosaur called Iguanodon had spikes instead of thumbs.

Fact: The jaws of a tyrannosaurus were so big that it could open its mouth more than a metre.

Fact: The ancestor of the horse, the dawn horse, was the size of a fox and had toes instead of hoofs.

Fact: Coelacanths are the only known survivors of a very ancient group of fishes. They were thought to have become extinct about 90 million years ago, but in 1938 one was caught in the Indian Ocean.

Fact: The largest flying creature that has ever existed was a pterosaur (flying reptile) with a wingspan of about 12 metres, bigger than a two-seater aeroplane.

Habitats

An animal's habitat is the place where it lives naturally. Animals live in almost every part of the world. Many are specially equipped for the areas in which they live. Some animals are naturally found in only one part of the world, but have been taken to other places by man.

1 Do all animals stay in one area?

2 Hippos live in rivers and lakes. In which continent would you find them?

3 Do any animals live in the Sahara Desert?

4 Only one monkey, the Barbary ape, lives wild in Europe. Where does it live?
- (a) In the mountains of Switzerland
- (b) In the Welsh valleys
- (c) On the rock of Gibraltar

5 Which of these animals lives both in the rain forest and out on the grassland (savannah)?
(a) The okapi
(b) The elephant
(c) The wild boar

6 In which of the following places might you find a black bear?
(a) The West Indies
(b) Canada
(c) The New Forest

7 How do most animals of the Australian desert cope with the high temperatures?
(a) By drinking a lot
(b) By staying in the shade
(c) By sleeping in the day and being active at night

8 In which country would you find wild budgerigars?
(a) Australia
(b) Russia
(c) Mexico

9 Where would you find an alligator?
(a) In a swamp
(b) In the desert
(c) Up a tree

10 Which of these animals is still found in Scotland?
  (a) The wild yak
  (b) The pine marten
  (c) The giant ant-eater

11 Which animals are best suited to desert life?
  (a) Mammals
  (b) Reptiles
  (c) Birds

12 Where do birds of paradise come from?
  (a) Cyprus
  (b) Japan
  (c) New Guinea

13 Which of these mammals lives at the greatest height above sea level?
  (a) The reindeer
  (b) The mountain goat
  (c) The yak

14 In tropical regions, what do monkeys, jackals and wild pigs go to the beach for?
   (a) To swim
   (b) To hunt for shrimps and crabs
   (c) To lick salt from the rocks

15 What is special about polar bears' feet that protects them from the cold and from slipping on ice?
   (a) They have horny scales
   (b) They are covered in fur
   (c) They have an extra layer of fat

16 Where did the pheasant originally come from?
   (a) China
   (b) Iceland
   (c) Russia

17 How long are the tropical wasps that are found in Malaysia and Indonesia?
   (a) 3 centimetres
   (b) 10 centimetres
   (c) 25 centimetres

18 Which is the biggest area of corals in the world?

19 Where would you find a kiwi?
   (a) Greenland
   (b) New Zealand
   (c) Peru

20 Where is the only place where you would find a lemur wild?
  (a) Greece
  (b) Egypt
  (c) Madagascar

21 Are all eighteen species of penguin found wild north or south of the equator?

22 What do mountain insects depend on for their food?
  (a) Birds
  (b) Mountain streams
  (c) The wind

23 Which fish would you find plenty of in summer in Arctic waters?
  (a) Herrings
  (b) Tench
  (c) Piranhas

Fact: Hippos were common in the Thames 100,000 years ago.

Fact: Animals that live high up (above sea level) often have stronger hearts and lungs because there is less oxygen. They also have thicker coats, to keep them warm and prevent the sun's ultra-violet rays, which are stronger higher up, from harming them.

Primates

**This is the 'first' group of animals because it includes
human beings, as well as apes, monkeys and lemurs.**

1 Which is the largest living primate?

2 How are the feet of gibbons, orang-utans and chimpanzees different from man's?

3 What is the difference between a monkey and an ape?

4 Of all the apes, which are called the 'lesser apes'?
 (a) Gibbons
 (b) Chimpanzees
 (c) Gorillas

5 Do gorillas walk on two legs or all fours?

6 Which monkeys might you find in a mangrove swamp?
 (a) Proboscis monkeys
 (b) Green monkeys
 (c) Pig-tailed macaques

7 Where do gibbons like to live?
 (a) On the prairie
 (b) In the rain forest
 (c) On the tundra

8 Gibbons use their arms to swing under branches. How far can they go in one swing?
   (a) 2 metres
   (b) 6 metres
   (c) 10 metres

9 Which primate has a red and blue nose and a bottom to match?
   (a) A lemur
   (b) A mandrill
   (c) A baboon

BLUSH!

10 Which monkey has no hair on its buttocks?

11 Which apes get up late and go to bed early?
   (a) Orang-utans
   (b) Gorillas
   (c) Chimpanzees

12 Which is the smallest monkey?
   (a) The spider monkey
   (b) The macaque
   (c) The marmoset

13 Which is the largest of the lesser apes?
   (a) The black gibbon
   (b) The siamang
   (c) The white-handed gibbon

14 All great apes build nests. How often do chimpanzees build them?
   (a) Once a week
   (b) Every day
   (c) Once a year

Fact: Gorillas have been seen to eat parts of over a hundred different types of plant.

Mammals

Mammals are animals which have fur or hair. They give birth to babies and feed them on their milk. They are warm-blooded, and so can control their body temperature. Like their nearest relatives, apes and monkeys, human beings are mammals.

1 The first mammals were small, like shrews. When did they first appear on earth?
  (a) About 7 million years ago
  (b) About 200 million years ago
  (c) About 350 million years ago

2 Which is the smallest mammal?
  (a) The pipistrelle bat
  (b) The harvest mouse
  (c) The Etruscan shrew

3 What type of animal are these: leopard, tiger, lion, jaguar, snow leopard?

4 What is a fox's tail called?

5 How much does a harvest mouse weigh?
   (a) 120 grams
   (b) 7 grams
   (c) 265 grams

6 What are deer's antlers covered with when they are newly grown?
   (a) Feathers
   (b) Velvet
   (c) Horn

7 Can hippopotamuses swim?

8 What is this?

9 Where does the animal in the drawing above live?
   (a) Russia
   (b) South America
   (c) Australia

10 How can you tell the difference between African and Indian elephants?

11 Which member of the cat family is best at jumping?
(a) The tiger
(b) The puma
(c) The jaguar

12 Which animal fells trees to build dams?

13 What is a moose?
(a) A duck
(b) A moth
(c) A deer

14 What are scavengers?
(a) Animals that eat birds' eggs
(b) Animals that eat what others leave behind
(c) Birds that hunt for insects on animals

15 Which is the only mammal that can kneel on all fours?

16 Why do camels have thick pads on their feet?
(a) to make them taller
(b) to protect their feet from hot sand
(c) so that their feet don't wear out on safari

17 Which are the only mammals that fly?

18 How long do mice usually live in the wild?
   (a) 1½ years
   (b) 6 years
   (c) 9½ years

19 How long can seals stay under water?
   (a) 4 minutes
   (b) 30 minutes
   (c) 2 hours

20 What is stored in a camel's hump?
   (a) Water
   (b) Fat
   (c) Blood

21 When a very thirsty camel gets water, how much can it drink in ten minutes?
  (a) 20 litres
  (b) 67 litres
  (c) 115 litres

22 Which has two humps – the Arabian or the Bactrian camel?

23 Why do most cats retract their claws?
  (a) So they won't trip over them
  (b) To keep them clean
  (c) So that they stay sharp

24 What do cats use to sharpen their claws?
  (a) Tree trunks
  (b) Their teeth
  (c) Gritty rocks

25 Can kangaroos swim?

26 Which squirrels have ear tufts – red or grey?

27 Which of these animals climb best?
  (a) Leopards
  (b) Lions
  (c) Tigers

28 Are otters active during the day or night?

29 There are about 950 different species of bat altogether. How many species are there in the British Isles?

30 What is the common name for the North American bison?

31 Which animals like to take a shower?

32 What is a dromedary?
   (a) A mountain goat
   (b) A one-humped Arabian camel
   (c) A sort of gazelle

33 There are two sorts of rat in Britain: the brown or common rat, and the black or ship's rat. Which lives upstairs and which lives downstairs?

Fact: Rodents gnaw their food, but their teeth don't wear right down as they are continually growing.

Fact: Polar bears are the most intelligent of their kind. They have been known to cover their conspicuous black noses with a paw when creeping up on a seal.

Fact: A human baby is usually born head first, but the calf or baby of a whale, dolphin or porpoise is usually born tail first.

Birds

Birds are two-legged animals with feathers and a beak. Most of them can fly. Males often have much more colourful plumage than females.

1 What were the ancestors of the birds?
- (a) Mammals
- (b) Insects
- (c) Reptiles

2 How many species of bird are there in the world?
- (a) 3,750
- (b) 8,580
- (c) 11,130

3 Can all birds fly?

4 Is a puffin's beak plain, striped or spotted?

5 What is the name of this bird, which has a big pouch under its bill to hold fish?

6 Which of these garden birds is the most common?
(a) The blackbird
(b) The house sparrow
(c) The blue tit

7 Which is the smallest bird in the world?
(a) The wren
(b) The bee hummingbird
(c) The goldcrest

8 What kind of beak would a seed-eating bird have?
(a) Thin and pointed
(b) Hooked
(c) Stout

9 Why do kingfishers swallow fish head first?
   (a) Because the head is tastiest
   (b) So the fish don't bite them
   (c) So the fish's scales don't stick in their throat

10 Which is the largest gull?

11 Which is the largest British bird of prey?

12 How many feathers do swans have?
   (a) About 400
   (b) About 7,000
   (c) About 25,000

13 Which is the world's fastest-running bird?

14 Which bird can walk under water?
   (a) The dipper
   (b) The oyster-catcher
   (c) The plover

15 Where does the elf owl live?
   (a) In the top branch of a pine tree
   (b) In a hole in a giant cactus
   (c) In a disused rabbit burrow

16 Which birds do you associate with the Tower of London?

17 Why is the flamingo's beak bent down?
    (a) To attract females
    (b) Because it is short-sighted
    (c) To catch food

18 Which have long, pointed wings: hawks, eagles or falcons?

19 Where do snowy owls breed?
    (a) In Austria
    (b) In the Arctic
    (c) In the Sahara Desert

20 Wild budgerigars have feathers of only one colour. Which is it?
 (a) Yellow
 (b) Blue
 (c) Green

21 Which of these birds can fly backwards?
 (a) Flycatchers
 (b) Wrens
 (c) Hummingbirds

22 Where do woodpeckers nest?
 (a) In a hawthorn hedge
 (b) Under the eaves of a house
 (c) In a hole in a tree trunk

23 How long does a robin usually live?
 (a) 13 months
 (b) 6½ years
 (c) 14 years

24 Which bird keeps a larder of spare food stuck on thorn bushes?
 (a) A shrike
 (b) A nuthatch
 (c) A flycatcher

25 Which living bird has the greatest wing-span?
 (a) The golden eagle
 (b) The Andean condor
 (c) The wandering albatross

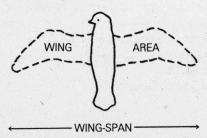

26 Which bird flies off with acorns and buries them, to eat later?
(a) The magpie
(b) The jay
(c) The lark

27 Why are vultures bald on their heads and necks?
(a) Because of old age
(b) Because they pull each other's feathers out
(c) So they don't get messy pulling meat out of carcasses

28 Name three kinds of tit.

29 How do nuthatches hold a nut steady while they break it open?
(a) Between their feet
(b) By wedging it in the bark of a tree
(c) By pressing it to the ground with their tummies

30 The male emperor penguin keeps the egg warm on his feet, covered by a flap of skin. How long does he have to stand like this before the egg hatches?
(a) 5 days
(b) 4 weeks
(c) 2 months

31 Which birds are pirates, taking fish that other birds have caught?
(a) Petrels
(b) Cormorants
(c) Skuas

32 Which (living) bird has the best sense of smell?
(a) A kiwi
(b) A lapwing
(c) A gannet

33 Why do ospreys drop into the water feet first?
(a) To soften their landing
(b) To keep their heads dry
(c) To catch fish just below the surface

34 Which bird has the most upturned bill?
(a) An avocet
(b) A woodcock
(c) A heron

35 Where do herons, avocets and wild duck like to build their nests?
(a) Among sand dunes
(b) On rock ledges
(c) On the marshes

36 How does the woodpecker finch remove insects and their larvae from the bark of trees?
(a) With its pointed beak
(b) By scraping with a cactus spine
(c) By scraping with its claws

37 What do these birds have in common: the king penguin, the cassowary and the emu?

38 Why is a missel-thrush sometimes called a 'storm-cock'?
(a) Because it sings in all weathers
(b) Because it prefers wet weather
(c) Because it spreads its wings if a storm is coming

39 Which birds cause problems at aerodromes?
(a) Gulls
(b) Owls
(c) Crows

Fact: Eagles can kill prey three or four times their own size.

Fact: The deepest-diving bird in the world is the emperor penguin, which has been recorded as diving 265 metres below the surface.

Fact: Most birds have three toes facing forwards and one backwards. The parrot family have two facing each way, which means they can grip very well.

Fact: Swallows fly with their beaks open to catch insects; they can also drink from the water's surface while flying along.

Fact: An owl's eyes are too large to swivel, so the whole head must be turned to see things.

Markings and Camouflage

Animals from one species all look basically the same, although there are often individual differences; for example, no two giraffes have exactly the same pattern. Males are often more brightly coloured than females, especially in the breeding season. Coats, eyes, feet and beaks are often specially suited to the way in which that particular animal lives; sometimes their appearance disguises them, like stick and leaf insects which are very difficult to see on small branches.

1 What does a bird have that no other animal has?

2 What is this?

3 Which male monkey has an enlarged nose?
   (a) The howler monkey
   (b) The proboscis monkey
   (c) The spider monkey

4 Which crab can stick pieces of seaweed or sponge on to its spiny shell to provide camouflage?
   (a) The velvet crab
   (b) The spider crab
   (c) The masked crab

5 How often do deer shed their antlers?

6 Which usually has a moist skin, an amphibian or a reptile?

7 Which has a black tip to its tail, a weasel or a stoat?

8 Which mammal has hair that lies the 'wrong way', that is, towards its head and the top of its back, rather than to its belly?
   (a) The raccoon
   (b) The sloth
   (c) The mongoose

9 Does a lobster's tough outer coat grow at the same rate as the lobster?

10 There are four sorts of zebra; how can you tell them apart?
- (a) By the shape of their ears
- (b) By the length of their tails
- (c) By the pattern of stripes on their bottoms

11 Which animal has its own ice-pick?
- (a) The Arctic fox
- (b) The walrus
- (c) The elephant seal

12 What is this?

13 Can you see any difference between a crocodile and an alligator?

14 Which male crab has one enormous pincer which it uses for fighting and to attract females?
- (a) The fiddler crab
- (b) The masked crab
- (c) The hermit crab

Fact: Mole fur can be brushed smoothly forwards or backwards.

Fact: Squids can change colour to match their surroundings.

Fact: Flamingos and canaries must eat the right food to stay brightly coloured. Their diet includes special crustacea and food containing 'carotenoids'.

Fact: Many insects and crustaceans have compound eyes, consisting of a great number (sometimes thousands) of minute simple eyes closely crowded together. The eyes can be very large in relation to the body – for example those of the house fly.

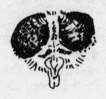

Reptiles

WOBBLE!

Reptiles are scaly, air-breathing creatures which move about on their bellies or on very short legs. They are cold-blooded, which means that their bodies are at the same temperature as their surroundings.

1 What is distinctive about a snake's tongue?

2 Why do crocodiles bask in the sun with their mouths open?
   (a) To get cool
   (b) To exercise their jaws
   (c) To catch food

3 Is a slow-worm a snake?

4 Which is the largest reptile in the world?
- (a) The estuarine crocodile
- (b) The hawksbill turtle
- (c) The chameleon

5 Is a snake's tongue poisonous?

6 Many iguanas live in trees and some can swim – what sort of reptiles are they?
- (a) Turtles
- (b) Lizards
- (c) Alligators

7 How did the rattlesnake get its name?

8 Why do snakes and some lizards flicker their tongues when active?
(a) To catch insects
(b) To help identify smells
(c) To lose excess heat

9 Which of these snakes kills animals by coiling round them and squeezing them so they cannot breathe?
(a) The green mamba
(b) The boa constrictor
(c) The python

10 Do reptiles breathe with lungs or gills?

11 Which is the largest living lizard?
(a) The gila monster
(b) The komodo dragon
(c) The frilled lizard

12 Gaboon vipers have venom glands which hold a lot of poison – enough to kill how many people?
(a) 3
(b) 7
(c) 12

13 Where do crocodiles and alligators spend the night?
(a) On rocks
(b) In caves
(c) In water

14 Three snakes are found in the British Isles; which is the odd one out: grass snake, sidewinder, adder (illustrated), smooth snake?

15 What do we call turtles that live on land all the time?
  (a) Tortoises
  (b) Terrapins
  (c) Tapirs

16 Why do crocodiles swallow stones?

17 Which of these snakes can grow the longest?
  (a) The reticulated python
  (b) The king cobra
  (c) The easter diamond-back rattlesnake

18 Which land snake has the most poisonous venom of all?
  (a) The rattlesnake
  (b) The tiger snake
  (c) The boomslang

Fact: While Nile crocodiles bask with their mouths open, birds such as spur-winged and Egyptian plovers clean their teeth for them.

Fact: Alligator and crocodile eggs have hard shells. The unborn young have a point on their heads to help them break out; this is called an 'egg tooth'.

Amphibians

The word amphibian comes from the Greek meaning 'double life'. Amphibians are born in the water. They can then live on land, but have to return to the water to breed.

1 What is the difference between the skin of a frog and that of a toad?

2 Which back leg of a common frog's tadpole's body grows first?

3 What do fire-bellied toads do if they are frightened?
   (a) Lie on their backs
   (b) Puff out steam
   (c) Dive into the water

4 What is a newt?
   (a) A kind of salamander
   (b) A tropical frog
   (c) A nocturnal lizard

5 Most salamanders are nocturnal. When are they most active?
   (a) After a hot day when the earth is warm
   (b) After rain
   (c) In the snow

6 How do tree frogs hold on?
   (a) With claws on their feet
   (b) With suckers on each toe
   (c) With hooked scales on their bellies

7 Some frogs and toads defend themselves by leaking smelly fluid through their skin. This is why one of these toads is known as the garlic toad. Which one?
(a) The yellow-bellied toad
(b) The European spade-foot
(c) The natterjack

8 The largest toad in the world is the South American giant toad. How long is it?
(a) 9 centimetres
(b) 17 centimetres
(c) 23 centimetres

9 Rain frogs sometimes eat so much that they expand like a ball and can hardly walk. What have they eaten?
(a) Slugs
(b) Snails
(c) Termites

Fact: When a frog or toad swallows food, it closes its eyes to help push the food from its mouth to its stomach.

Insects

There are more types of insect than all other species of animal put together. They have a body with a clearly divided head, thorax and abdomen; many have wings.

1 What name is given to the pair of feelers on an insect's head?

2 How many legs do insects have?
  (a) 8
  (b) 4
  (c) 6

3 What is this?

4 Do dragonflies close their wings when they are resting?

5 What is the name given to shedding a skin?

6 How many times does a young grasshopper change its skin
as it grows up?
(a) 5 or 6 times
(b) Twice
(c) Not at all

7 What are male bees called?

8 What do dung beetles do with their eggs after they are laid?
(a) Cover them with leaves
(b) Press them into a crevice in a tree
(c) Roll them in a ball of dung and bury it

9 What is another name for the daddy-long-legs?

10 Which is the longest British beetle?
(a) The devil's coach-horse
(b) The cockchafer
(c) The stag beetle

11 Which of these British beetles eats wood?
   (a) The tiger beetle
   (b) The colorado beetle
   (c) The death-watch beetle

12 Which insect dies when it has used its sting?

13 Which of these diseases can be carried by mosquitoes in warm areas of the world?
   (a) Measles
   (b) Whooping cough
   (c) Malaria

14 Why do ants rub their antennae together when they meet?
   (a) To transfer pollen
   (b) To find out if they are from the same nest
   (c) To keep their antennae clean

15 Which insects grow gardens of fungi inside their nests?
   (a) Termites
   (b) Stick insects
   (c) Cockroaches

Fact: Some insects are cannibals. The female praying mantis sometimes eats the male.

Fact: Grasshoppers make their sound by rubbing their hind legs or a leg and a wing together.

Fact: When locusts migrate after breeding, their swarms are so huge that when they feed they can devastate entire crops.

Spiders

Spiders have a head and thorax joined together, and an abdomen. They have eight legs. They all spin silk and are predatory, feeding mostly on insects. Females are usually bigger than males.

1 Is a spider an insect?

2 Which is the largest British spider?
   (a) The spitting spider
   (b) The raft spider
   (c) The pirate spider

3 How many eyes do most spiders have?
   (a) 2
   (b) 8
   (c) 24

4 Spider silk or thread is very light. How much would a strand that went right round the world weigh?
(a) Less than 50 grams
(b) Less than 170 grams
(c) Less than 500 grams

5 How many species of spider are there in Britain?
(a) 15
(b) 120
(c) Over 600

6 The bolas spider from the southern United States catches moths. How?
(a) By making a huge web
(b) By jumping on them
(c) By throwing a sticky blob on a line at the moth

7 What does the female black widow spider often do after mating?
(a) She goes to sleep
(b) She gets a meal for the male
(c) She eats the male

8 Why do web spiders get excited if their web vibrates?
(a) Because they like music
(b) Because they think they have caught a meal
(c) Because they think it is going to rain

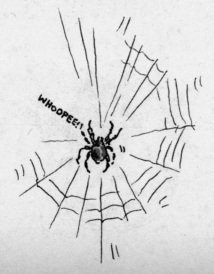

9 How do house spiders often get into houses?
  (a) Through key holes
  (b) Up the bath waste-pipe
  (c) Down the chimney

10 Which of these is the most venomous?
  (a) The garden spider
  (b) The black widow
  (c) The wolf spider

11 Can the bite of any British spider kill a person?

12 What happens to a jumping spider if it falls?
  (a) It rolls into a ball so it bounces
  (b) It is caught by a safety rope
  (c) It is so light that it drifts down like a feather

Fact: In Thailand, people toast and eat edible spiders. They are said to taste like chicken.

Butterflies and Moths

These form the insect group Lepidoptera – 'scale winged'. Their wings and bodies are covered in tiny scales which make up their colour patterns. Butterflies come out in the day and are usually more colourful than moths, which fly at night.

1 One of these descriptions fits a butterfly, the other a moth. Which is which?
   (a) Furry body, feathered antennae, wings folded upright on landing
   (b) Thin, smooth body, thin antennae with a blob on the end, wings usually spread on landing

2 Before a butterfly or moth can hatch, it goes through three stages: chrysalis, egg and caterpillar. Put them in their correct order.

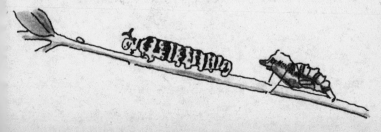

3 Which of the following is a butterfly?
  (a) Semi-colon
  (b) Comma
  (c) Capital letter

4 What does the garden-white butterfly like to feed on?
  (a) Tomatoes
  (b) Runner beans
  (c) Cabbage

5 Are there more species of butterflies or moths in Britain?

6 Which of these flower names is also the name of a butterfly?
  (a) Fritillary
  (b) Buttercup
  (c) Polyanthus

7 What is a 'woolly bear'?

8 The colour in the name of one of these butterflies is wrong:
  which one, and what should it be?
  (a) Yellow tip
  (b) Purple emperor
  (c) Red admiral

9 Which British moth larva spins a silk cocoon?

10 The following are all one sort of moth: death's head, hummingbird, privet. Which are they?
    (a) Hawk-moths
    (b) Tiger-moths
    (c) Micro-moths

11 What juice do butterflies and moths get from flowers?

12 Butterflies are cold-blooded. Where does the heat come from that activates them to fly?

13 Which moth has the name of an animal (beginning with E) and of a bird (beginning with H) in its name?

14 What is a burnished brass?
    (a) A butterfly
    (b) A moth
    (c) A dragonfly

15 Where does the red admiral butterfly lay its eggs?
    (a) On the underside of oak leaves
    (b) On nettles
    (c) In crevices in walls

16 Which of these bird names is also the name of a butterfly?
    (a) Petrel
    (b) Peacock
    (c) Plover

17 How can procession moth caterpillars, which eat pine needles and harm the trees, be controlled?
(a) By spraying with chemicals
(b) By releasing flocks of finches to eat them
(c) By encouraging red ants to live there

18 What sort of butterfly are the following: pearl bordered, dark green and Queen of Spain?
(a) Brown butterflies
(b) Fritillary butterflies
(c) Heath butterflies

19 Male moths that fly at night can scent females with their sensitive feathered antennae up to how far away?
(a) 5 feet
(b) 5 yards
(c) 5 miles

20 What do silk worms (larvae of the silk moth) feed on?
(a) Beech leaves
(b) Pine needles
(c) Mulberry leaves

21 The purple emperor is a rare butterfly. Where would you hope to see one?
(a) On chalk downland
(b) In apple orchards
(c) Around the tops of forest oak trees

22 When did the large blue butterfly become extinct in Britain?
   (a) 1963
   (b) 1979
   (c) 1981

Fact: Some caterpillars, like that of the puss-moth, can scare away predators by making frightening faces!

Fish

Fish are cold-blooded animals with backbones and fins. They live in fresh or salt water and breathe through gills.

1 Most fish have two pairs of nostrils; what are they used for?
 (a) Breathing
 (b) Smelling the water
 (c) Hearing echoes

2 Where do fish live in the greatest numbers?
 (a) On the seabed
 (b) In fast-flowing rivers
 (c) Around coral reefs

3 Which is the odd fish out and why?
 (a) Cod
 (b) Herring
 (c) Perch

4 What is this?

DORSAL FINS

TAIL FIN

PECTORAL FIN

5 Which of these fins do which job?

6 Which is the biggest shark?
   (a) The basking shark
   (b) The leopard shark
   (c) The whale shark

7 Which of these fish grows the biggest?
   (a) The minnow
   (b) The salmon
   (c) The trout

8 Which fish likes to have its teeth cleaned?
   (a) The basking shark
   (b) The barracuda
   (c) The pike

9 What is a crayfish?

10 Which is the most venomous fish around Britain?
   (a) The cod
   (b) The mackerel
   (c) The weever

11 Which fish has scales the size of saucers?
   (a) The halibut
   (b) The perch
   (c) The tarpon

12 Which fish is which? Clown-fish, Sweetlips, Snapper.

13 What is a large group of fish called?

14 Where do piranha fish live wild?
  (a) In the Thames
  (b) In South American rivers
  (c) In the sea

15 Flat-fish are usually lazy, so they are good at camouflage which gives them a better chance of surviving. Where would you find a plaice?
  (a) Near the surface of the water
  (b) On the seabed
  (c) Around coral reefs

16 What do several types of Amazonian fish eat?
  (a) Coral
  (b) Plankton
  (c) Fruit

17 Which fish hides and then pounces on smaller fish and eats them?
  (a) The grayling
  (b) The stickleback
  (c) The pike

18 How do Arctic cod stand the cold?
  (a) They have very thick skins
  (b) They have antifreeze in their blood
  (c) They have a layer of blubber or fat

19 Do fish have eyelids?

20 What is this?

21 How do salmon navigate across the ocean?
  (a) Using the sun and stars
  (b) By temperature
  (c) By smell

22 What are the eggs of fish called?

23 Which is the only flat-fish to live in fresh water in Britain?
  (a) The plaice
  (b) The flounder
  (c) The skate

24 Which is the biggest ray?
   (a) The manta ray
   (b) The Pacific ray
   (c) The eagle ray

25 Are sharks more likely to attack humans in warm or cold water?

26 Which fish eat coral?
   (a) Clown-fish
   (b) Red mullet
   (c) Parrot-fish

27 Which fish was thought to be extinct and then reappeared?
   (a) The tuna
   (b) The coelacanth
   (c) The sturgeon

28 Which fish can jump, crawl and climb?
   (a) The flying fish
   (b) The bass
   (c) The mudskipper

29 These freshwater fish are found around Britain. Which is the largest?
(a) The carp
(b) The minnow
(c) The trout

30 Which fish has a sucker round its mouth, by which it attaches itself to other fish and drinks their blood?
(a) The lamprey
(b) The catfish
(c) The mackerel

31 What is this?

32 The African lungfish can survive if the water dries up because it can breathe air. How long can it wait for water?
(a) 10 hours
(b) 23 days
(c) 5 years

33 What is a lateral line?
(a) The point where freshwater rivers meet the sea
(b) A line of nerve-endings along the side of most fish which helps them to judge distance
(c) A line of teeth-like marks on a shark's tail to confuse prey

34 Which fish are often found around old wrecks?
(a) Pollack
(b) Sea bream
(c) Grey mullet

Fact: Some fish that live at great depths are luminous.

Fact: Electric eels use the electricity they produce to help find their way about in muddy water.

Fact: The most poisonous fish in the world is the Japanese puffer-fish. The spiky puffer-fish can gulp in water or air if it is frightened to make it blow up like a ball.

Fact: Salmon travel downriver to the sea and then back upriver to breed. Eels live in rivers and go out to sea to breed.

Fact: Although small, rarely reaching 60 centimetres in length, piranha fish are able to overcome and devour large animals, and even human beings, by sheer weight of numbers.

Nocturnal Animals

These are animals that sleep during the day, and become active at night.

1 How might you guess that a bushbaby is a nocturnal animal?

2 Which nocturnal animal rolls itself into a prickly ball for protection?

3 Which bird is famous for its night song?
  (a) The oriole
  (b) The warbler
  (c) The nightingale

4 Can a long-eared owl hear better than a short-eared owl?

5 How do bats sleep?

6 Which of these comes out on wet days or at night, and eats fungi?
- (a) The grass snake
- (b) The slug
- (c) The barn owl

7 Do flying foxes (fruit-bats) navigate by sight or by sound?

8 Which crab comes on to tropical beaches at night?
- (a) The shore crab
- (b) The ghost crab
- (c) The hermit crab

9 What does an aardvark use to catch termites?
- (a) Its nose
- (b) Its big claws
- (c) Its tongue

10 Where do most scorpions spend the day?
- (a) Sunbathing on a rock
- (b) Sleeping in deep burrows
- (c) At the bottom of small pools

11 Which is the smallest British bat?
   (a) The natterer's bat
   (b) The pipistrelle
   (c) The whiskered bat

12 Which is the only monkey that is active at night?
   (a) The green monkey
   (b) The owl monkey
   (c) The howler monkey

13 Bechstein's bat is the rarest bat in Britain. Where would you be most likely to find one?
   (a) The Isle of Skye
   (b) The Brecon Beacons
   (c) The New Forest

14 How many species of owl are there?
   (a) Over 200
   (b) 27
   (c) 9

15 Which nocturnal animal digs small pits outside its home to use as a toilet?
   (a) A hare
   (b) A weasel
   (c) A badger

16 How do spiny ant-eaters groom themselves?
  (a) By pushing their way through bushes
  (b) With two big claws on their hind legs
  (c) By running their long noses through each other's hair
      and quills

Fact: Fruit-bats roost by day in caves and trees, sometimes in
flocks of many thousands.

Fact: The largest measured wing-span for a bat is 1.7 metres.

Fact: The speckled jellyfish and the rosebud jellyfish glow in
the dark.

Winter Changes

Animals cope with winter in various ways. Some change their coats; others, like bears, sleep through it all. Several move to warmer places, sometimes covering great distances.

1 What is the name given to the long winter sleep that some animals take?

2 What is the name given to the long journey that some birds make in the summer and winter?

3 Where do most frogs spend the winter?
   (a) Under a pile of leaves
   (b) In the mud at the bottom of a pond
   (c) In a nest among rushes

4 Which kind of butterfly migrates in its millions to mountains near Mexico City for the winter?

5 How often do hibernating animals eat?
   (a) Once a day
   (b) Once a week
   (c) Not at all

6 Which bird migrates furthest?
   (a) The Arctic tern
   (b) The swallow
   (c) The cuckoo

7 Do all birds of the same species winter in the same place?

8 Some turtles have recently been found to hibernate. Where do they do this?
   (a) In a pit dug on a sandy shore
   (b) In a cave
   (c) On the seabed

9 A puffin's feet are red in the summer; what colour are they in the winter?
(a) Blue
(b) Yellow
(c) Purple

10 Where do the large plankton-feeding whales spend the summer?
(a) In tropical waters
(b) In polar waters

11 Where does the cuckoo spend the winter?
(a) Australia
(b) Africa
(c) The West Indies

12 What do groups of wild boar mainly live on during the winter on the plains?
(a) Fat
(b) Insects
(c) Plants

13 What do the ptarmigan, the mountain hare and the stoat do to hide themselves in the winter snows?
  (a) Hibernate under a rock
  (b) Grow a new, white coat
  (c) Move about only at night

14 Where do rock-hoppers, sooty albatrosses and skuas spend the summer?
  (a) The Galapagos Islands
  (b) Tenerife
  (c) Antarctica

Fact: Musk deer live in Asia. They have thick wavy hair which is filled with pockets of air so the snow doesn't melt through.

Hunting

Predators – animals that eat other animals – must first catch their prey. Some have weapons like claws or poison fangs to help them, while others must set a trap.

1 Which fish shoots out water drops to dislodge insects from plants?
  (a) The stingray
  (b) The archer-fish
  (c) The trigger-fish

2 Do badgers hunt for food during the day or night?

3 Seals come up through holes in the ice to breathe. Which animal might be lying in wait, hoping to catch and eat them?
  (a) A walrus
  (b) A killer whale
  (c) A polar bear

4 How does the ant-lion catch ants?
(a) By dropping on to them from a rock
(b) By digging a sandpit for them to fall into
(c) By squirting them with sticky liquid

5 Which animal could catch and eat a hummingbird?
(a) A chameleon
(b) A tarantula
(c) A marmoset

6 Do male or female lions do the hunting?

7 Jackals, hyenas and vultures eat the remains of animals that have been killed by others. Where would a tiger hide his kill?
(a) Up a tree
(b) Under a pile of leaves
(c) Under the ground

8 What has eight arms and can hide by changing its colour, before striking very fast?

9 What do wolves hunt for?
(a) Moose and caribou
(b) Rodents and birds
(c) Fish

10 Which bird stirs up the water and spreads its wings to trick
fish into swimming under their shade for safety?
(a) The reddish egret
(b) The great blue heron
(c) The Andean flamingo

11 How do rattlesnakes find their prey in the dark?
(a) They can sense the heat of warm-blooded creatures
(b) Their eyes are specially equipped for night vision
(c) They wait outside burrows they have seen during the
day

12 Peregrine falcons dive down on their prey at up to 240
kilometres per hour, killing it on impact. What is this called?
(a) Diving
(b) Plunging
(c) Stooping

Fact: Some pelicans have a very effective method of catching
fish. They swim along in a tight line, pushing the fish
towards the bank, and then all plunge their beaks in
together.

Fact: The greatest ratter was a bull terrier bitch called Jenny
Lind who killed 500 rats in 1½ hours in Liverpool.

Eating Habits

All animals eat plants or other animals. Eating habits often form 'food chains', for example plants are eaten by rabbits, rabbits are eaten by foxes, then the fox's dung (and eventually its dead body) feeds tiny soil creatures which produce the food to make plants grow.

1 What do koala bears eat?
(a) Honey
(b) Eucalyptus leaves
(c) Bananas

2 What is a carnivorous animal?

3 Do all carnivores eat only meat?

4 The harpy eagle which lives in the South American rain forest is the largest-known bird of prey. What does it eat?
  (a) Monkeys
  (b) Fruit
  (c) Insects

5 Do snakes eat their food whole or in parts?

6 Do clothes-moths eat clothes?

7 What internal part of a bird grinds up food?
  (a) The beak
  (b) The gizzard
  (c) Teeth

8 What do emus eat?
  (a) Lizards
  (b) Fish
  (c) Berries

Eating Habits 129

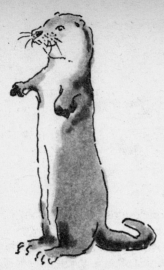

9 Why must otters eat some oily food?

10 Which bat drinks the blood of its victim?

11 What does a grasshopper eat?
    (a) Bugs
    (b) Greenfly
    (c) Grass

12 Which animal eats the bark of conifers?
    (a) The North American porcupine
    (b) The brown bear
    (c) The coyote

13 Some ants keep 'cows'. True or false?

14 Which of the following stores its food in pouches in its cheeks?
    (a) The beaver
    (b) The chipmunk
    (c) The raccoon

15 What is the main food of sperm whales?
   (a) Seaweed
   (b) Squid
   (c) Herrings

16 What does 'chewing the cud' mean?

17 How many chambers are there in a giraffe's stomach?
   (a) 7
   (b) 1
   (c) 4

18 Do both male and female mosquitoes live on blood?

19 Black and white rhinoceroses live in Africa. What do they eat?

20 What is the diet of squirrels, opossums and chipmunks living in Alaska?
   (a) Peanuts
   (b) Tea-leaves
   (c) Pine-cones

21 Which of these animals climbs to the top of coconut palms to open the nuts and feed on the pulp?
   (a) The woolly monkey
   (b) The robber crab
   (c) The toucan

22 What does the European thrush use to break open a snail shell?
   (a) Its beak
   (b) Its wing
   (c) A stone

23 Which of these parrots lives in New Zealand and can kill sheep?
  (a) The St Lucia parrot
  (b) The kea
  (c) The macaw

24 The individual man-eating record is held by a tigress called the 'Champawat man-eater'. How many people did she kill?
  (a) 17
  (b) 56
  (c) 438

Fact: Giraffes drink at irregular intervals. They can live on the moisture in leaves for weeks at a time.

Fact: Gorillas and chimpanzees suffer from tooth decay because of all the vegetation and (in the case of chimpanzees) fruit they eat.

Fact: Elephants use their tusks for digging up grass and roots to eat.

Fact: The African egg-eating snake eats birds' eggs whole. They are crushed as they are swallowed and the shells are later regurgitated.

Defence

Animals defend themselves from predators in many clever ways, and also protect their homes carefully. Creatures that are not well armed are often able to match the colour of their surroundings. Various fish like plaice can hardly be seen lying on the seabed, whereas other animals, which are poisonous or taste nasty (like the kingfisher), warn of their presence with a bright, exotic coat.

1 Why is the plateau of the Himalayas a good place for hoofed animals to live?
- (a) Because no predators can climb high enough to reach them
- (b) Because it's too cold for predators
- (c) Because they can see predators in time to avoid them

2 How do some frogs and toads defend themselves from snakes?
- (a) By spitting
- (b) By inflating themselves
- (c) By croaking loudly

3 What do millipedes have down each side of their body to
keep away enemies?
  (a) Sharp scales
  (b) Stink glands
  (c) Poisonous hairs

4 Which animal beats its chest to scare other animals away?

5 Where do some birds and kangaroo-rats nest to keep away
predators?
  (a) On very thin branches
  (b) Among clumps of cactus
  (c) On islands

6 How do some grass snakes protect themselves?
  (a) By pretending to be dead
  (b) By biting with poison fangs
  (c) By using the sting in their tail

7 What does a squid do when it needs to escape?

8 How does an antelope defend itself?
  (a) By biting its enemy with its poison fangs
  (b) By squeezing the enemy to suffocate it
  (c) By running away

9 Which mammal wears a suit of armour?
   (a) The springbok
   (b) The dromedary
   (c) The armadillo

10 How do many lizards escape death?
   (a) By eating their attacker
   (b) By diving under water
   (c) By shedding their tail

11 How does the black-necked cobra defend itself?
   (a) By remaining motionless
   (b) By pretending its tail is its head
   (c) By squirting venom into the eyes of its enemy

12 When termites are transporting food, they put soldiers out as guards along the line. How are the soldiers armed?
  (a) With a stick
  (b) With a nozzle on their heads that shoots out a sticky repellent
  (c) With sharp pincers on their front legs

Fact: Sea birds like gulls, puffins and guillemots form big colonies to nest which deter predators from stealing the eggs.

Fact: North American bobwhite birds settle for the night in a circle. This keeps them warm, and if a predator comes they all take off in different directions.

Animals in Danger

Sometimes animal species die out from natural causes as the dinosaurs did, but more often their decline is caused by human activities. They are hunted for meat, skin and other products, and their habitats are destroyed by building, agriculture and pollution.

1 How many kinds of animal are presently in danger of becoming extinct?
  (a) Over 1,000
  (b) Under 10
  (c) Over 150

2 What is conservation?

3 Which of these apes living in Borneo and Sumatra are becoming increasingly rare?
  (a) Gorillas
  (b) Orang-utans
  (c) Gibbons

4 Birds like egrets were once threatened by the demand for their plumage. This is no longer allowed. What were the feathers used for?
(a) Feather dusters
(b) Filling quilts
(c) Hats

5 Which animal's fur has become popular since restrictions have been imposed on protected species?
(a) The bear
(b) The wolf
(c) The fox

6 Which marine animals are hunted for meat and oil?

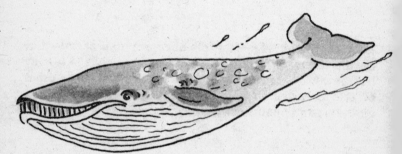

7 Which is the most threatened species of whale?
(a) The blue whale
(b) The grey whale
(c) The sperm whale

8 Which animal is endangered because its skin is used to make suitcases?
(a) The elephant
(b) The crocodile
(c) The armadillo

9 Where have vast national parks been made to protect animals like giraffes, rhinoceroses and elands?
  (a) The savannah areas of Africa
  (b) The bamboo forests of China
  (c) The high plateau of the Himalayas

10 What is this?

11 Like the golden eagle, the red kite is now protected to stop it dying out. Where does it live?
  (a) The Outer Hebrides
  (b) Central Wales
  (c) The Norfolk marshes

12 Which is the rarest British mammal?

13 One of the following deer died out in the Scottish Highlands in the twelfth century. It was reintroduced in the Cairngorms in 1952. Which is it?
   (a) Roe deer
   (b) Red deer
   (c) Reindeer

14 Why did the dodo become extinct?
   (a) Because it couldn't fly
   (b) Because it ran out of food
   (c) Because it didn't lay any eggs that year (1693)

15 Rain forests in South America, the habitat of tamarins and marmosets, are being continuously destroyed. How often do approximately 30 hectares (about the size of London Zoo) disappear?
   (a) Every year
   (b) Every week
   (c) Every minute

16 The brown bear is now very rare, but where can you still find it?
   (a) Canada
   (b) Russia
   (c) Norway

17 What kills thousands of water-birds each year?
   (a) Lack of food
   (b) Gales
   (c) Discarded fishing tackle

18 How do tse-tse flies help preserve the natural habitat?
   (a) They pollinate the flowers
   (b) They carry disease
   (c) They eat locusts

19 What are Red Data Books?
   (a) Lists of animals with red fur or feathers
   (b) Books describing animals and plants in danger of extinction
   (c) Lists of record measurements of animals

Fact: A hundred years ago when Mississippi alligators were common, they were found measuring up to 5.8 metres. Now it is rare to find one longer than 3.6 metres.

Fact: The Himalayan musk deer is in danger of extinction because it is hunted for its musk which is used in perfumes, cosmetics and oriental medicines.

Fact: Oil can pollute areas of the sea or beach. Birds get covered in it and seals die if they try to lick it off their bodies.

Animals and their Uses

Animals are used by man in many ways: for food – meat, fish, and also milk and eggs; skins and wool for warmth. Horses, donkeys, camels and other animals are used for transport. The study of animals can tell us many new things, for example how birds can find their way and fly so far. Animals also give great pleasure as pets.

1 How many pints of milk does a Friesian cow give per day (on average)?
(a) 4 pints
(b) 17 pints
(c) 35 pints

2 Which animals are the world's greatest meat producers?
   (a) Cattle
   (b) Sheep
   (c) Pigs

3 Which animal provides us with woolly jumpers?

4 How many sides do the wax cells of a honeycomb have?
   (a) 4
   (b) 6
   (c) 8

5 In which country are elephants trained to move trees?
   (a) Sweden
   (b) India
   (c) Canada

6 What is mutton?

7 Which vegetables grow well in horse manure?
   (a) Carrots
   (b) Lettuces
   (c) Mushrooms

8 Which animal are sausages made from?
   (a) Sheep
   (b) Chickens
   (c) Pigs

9 Which duck's feathers can be made into a very warm quilt?
   (a) The mallard
   (b) The tufted duck
   (c) The eider duck

10 Is bird-nest soup really made from birds' nests?

11 Which animal is used for transport in the desert?
   (a) The elephant
   (b) The donkey
   (c) The camel

12 Many wild animals are sold as pets. How many wild birds
   does India export each year?
   (a) About 20,000
   (b) About 200,000
   (c) About 2 million

13 What is venison?
  (a) Meat from sheep
  (b) Meat from deer
  (c) Meat from calves

14 What are rhino horns used for in West Asia?
  (a) Drinking cups
  (b) Dagger handles
  (c) Table legs

15 What did the domestic chicken that we eat so much of develop from?
  (a) The pelican
  (b) The jungle fowl
  (c) The wood pigeon

16 Why might dentists be interested in barnacles?
  (a) Because they have long-lasting teeth
  (b) Because their shells have an enamel coating
  (c) Because they can cling so tightly to the bottom of a boat

17 What do Amazonian Indians use on the tips of their poison-arrows?
   (a) Poison from the skin of tree frogs
   (b) Poison from the fangs of the pit viper
   (c) Venom from a hunting wasp's sting

18 Some animals can give us things we don't want; mosquitoes carry the disease malaria. Where might you catch it?
   (a) Scotland
   (b) India
   (c) Canada

19 Which wild animal is eaten most in Ghana (part of Africa)?
   (a) The giant rat
   (b) The bushbuck
   (c) The green monkey

20 Insects are underrated as food; many native people eat them. Where would you find deep-fried grasshopper for sale?
   (a) Australia
   (b) Malaysia
   (c) Peru

21 Grasshoppers are the most popular insect for eating. Which is the next favourite?
   (a) Termites
   (b) Praying mantis
   (c) Hawk-moths

22 Birds that fly great distances when migrating (like the stormy petrel and the albatross) provide useful information about one of these human ailments. Which?
   (a) Heart disease
   (b) Headaches
   (c) Pulled muscles

23 Crossing wild animals with domestic ones can sometimes be helpful. In California domestic cattle have been crossed with another animal, creating a breed that lives on grass alone without expensive extra food. Which animal were the cattle crossed with?
(a) The moose
(b) The wild antelope
(c) The bison

24 Which animal has recently been domesticated in Chile, so that it can be farmed?
(a) The wild toad
(b) The sealion
(c) The crocodile

25 Many developing countries earn money from fishing. What is the main catch that India, Thailand and Mexico sell?
(a) Sardines
(b) Cod
(c) Shrimps

26 Animals are very valuable for testing vaccines and other medicines. Which is most commonly used?
(a) The rhesus monkey
(b) The Indian rhinoceros
(c) The pygmy shrew

27 The majority of tropical fish sold for aquariums are wild ones. Where do most of these come from?
(a) South America
(b) Australia
(c) Scandinavia

28 Which animal does ivory come from?
    (a) Mountain goats
    (b) Elephants
    (c) Antelope

29 In Thailand people eat beetle larvae fried with salt. What are they supposed to taste like?
    (a) Shrimps
    (b) Raw potato and lettuce
    (c) Rice and sweetcorn

30 Which bird may be helpful to the design of crash helmets?
    (a) The cockatoo
    (b) The macaw
    (c) The woodpecker

31 Venom is often used in medicine. From which of the following is venom used in the treatment of arthritis?
    (a) The bee
    (b) The rattlesnake
    (c) The tarantula

DISH OF THE DAY

butterflies and moths ~ lightly ~ toasted ~

32 Where are lightly toasted butterflies and moths a favourite food?
(a) Bali
(b) Greenland
(c) Corsica

33 What have Californians started to use to clear the weed from their canals, replacing machines costing $500,000 a year?
(a) Eels
(b) Hippopotamuses
(c) Fish

34 Fungal infections like those following burns can be prevented by the use of an enzyme found in chitin. Where is chitin found?
(a) The horns of deer
(b) The shells of ostrich eggs
(c) The skeletons of crabs

35 Many animals are useful for monitoring the conditions of their surroundings. Clams and oysters filter water through their bodies every day, so they can be studied to see if they have chemicals, etc., in their bodies. How much water goes through their bodies every day?
(a) 20 pints (11 litres)
(b) 70 gallons (318 litres)
(c) 400 gallons (1820 litres)

Fact: In Bolivia, the export of skins of spotted cats and others is illegal, but a hunter can get more for one jaguar's skin than a year's income from farming.

Fact: In early America, white men and Indians used strings of shells and beads as money.

THE ANSWERS

Animal Homes (pp. 11–14)

1 An eyrie
2 A warren
3 (c) A squirrel
4 (c) A holt
5 (c) The stork
6 (b) The tailorbird
7 (b) Dry fish bones
8 (a) The house martin
9 (c) A beaver
10 (c) A set
11 (a) A lair
12 (b) Up to 8 metres
13 (c) Red squirrels

Families (pp. 15–20)

1 (b) 1
2 Tadpoles
3 Pythons; boas give birth to living young
4 Lambs
5 (c) A baby hare; a baby swan is a cygnet and a baby otter is a cub
6 (b) For the first three months they stay in a den hugging their mother to keep warm
7 The platypus and the spiny anteater
8 Fry
9 A joey
10 (b) 6 months
11 No, not for about three weeks
12 (c) 2–3 years
13 A cub
14 (c) The Asiatic elephant. She carries her baby for just over 20 months
15 (c) The male fighting fish makes the bubble nest, persuades a female to lay some eggs and then carries them in his mouth to the nest
16 The cuckoo
17 (c) On their mothers' backs
18 No. They are surrounded by a layer of jelly
19 Panda
20 Kittens

21 Two
22 Yes
23 They have to be kept warm to hatch
24 (c) About six years
25 The male
26 A foal
27 (a) Koalas
28 (b) The kiwi
29 (c) She leaves them hanging up
30 (b) They scurry into the sea before they can be picked up by predators

Living Together (pp. 21–7)

1 (c) A troop
2 A boomer
3 A cat
4 A pride
5 (b) It is calling out. It inflates the floor of its mouth to magnify the sound
6 (b) A charm
7 (c) He stares fiercely at them
8 (c) A school
9 Pandas live alone, except when they meet in the breeding season
10 Cocks and hens
11 The peacock
12 (b) A young pike
13 (b) A polecat. A female ferret is also called a Jill
14 (b) The superb lyrebird.
15 (b) By throwing a tantrum. Whoever makes the most noise – by screaming and throwing things like rocks around – becomes leader
16 (a) A male ferret. Male stoats and weasels are called dogs
17 A goat
18 (b) To attract females. After the breeding season they go back to normal
19 (b) A cat
20 (c) The hornbill. He walls up the entrance with mud, leaving a narrow slit to pass food in
21 A Jenny
22 Females
23 (b) A swarm. This collective noun also applies to bees
24 (a) Wrapped round his back legs

25 (c) Seals
26 A boar
27 (c) So it doesn't roll away when the parents change places
28 A vixen

Animal Bodies (pp. 28–33)

1 Vertebrates; invertebrates are animals without backbones
2 Yes
3 A skeleton
4 The rhinoceros. Indian and Javan rhinoceroses have two horns
5 It is fastened at the front, not the back, of the mouth
6 The porcupine
7 8
8 (a) Mammals
9 No. They have flippers
10 (c) 60–70 years
11 (a) 4. They are replaced six times by other teeth growing from 'buds' at the back
12 To keep sand out of their eyes in the desert
13 Yes. Boa constrictors and pythons have small claws on their underside; these are all that remain of the legs their ancestors had
14 (c) The Indian buffalo. Its horns can measure 2 metres from tip to tip
15 (c) The bat
16 (c) A spectacle
17 (b) 7
18 No. They all start life with about 6 pairs, but when adult they have between 15 and 177 pairs
19 No
20 On the middle of its body
21 (c) At least 12 millimetres
22 No. The earliest horses had fingers with large nails
23 (c) A chameleon

Domestic Animals (pp. 34–40)

1 (c) The husky
2 (b) The turkey
3 (a) The Persian
4 (b) The Shetland
5 Chickens
6 Pink
7 Shut. They don't open for several days

8 (a) Syria. A mother and twelve babies were found in Syria in 1930, and all our pets are descendants of these
9 A fleece
10 (c) St Bernards
11 (c) A cold
12 (b) Mexico
13 (b) A cow
14 (b) China and Japan
15 (c) 4,000 years
16 Siamese
17 Homing pigeons. They are taken miles from home and then released. They race home, finding their way instinctively
18 A cat
19 (b) A high quality dog whose family can be traced
20 They are all types of cattle
21 (b) To make them lighter for swimming. Poodles were originally used as gundogs for duck shooting. Their coats were trimmed so that the wet fur did not drag them down, but areas were left unclipped to protect their heart, lungs and legs
22 (b) They can breathe better standing up
23 (a) The chow
24 (b) The shepherd catches its hind leg or neck with a crook – a long stick with a curved end
25 (c) 34
26 (b) Moving sheep
27 (c) Dalmatians
28 (c) 21.1 hands (2.16 metres)
29 The tortoise

Signs and Footprints (pp. 41–4)

1 (b) A squirrel
2 (b) Runs
3 (a) An otter
4 (c) A wood-mouse
5 (c) Money spiders. There are about 250 sorts of money spiders in Britain
6 (b) Crotties. Hares' droppings are called currants; otters' are called spraints
7 (a) The dormouse
8 (c) A slug. The other two would have left teeth marks
9 (b) A fox

10 A mallard, which is the commonest duck in Britain
11 (a) Dog (b) Cat – the cat's has no claw prints
12 A house mouse – notice the tail drag
13 A pig
14 A rabbit going fast. If it was hopping slowly, the fore feet would be in front of the hind feet

On the Seashore (pp. 45–51)

1 (c) A crab
2 (a) Clinging to a rock
3 A sea urchin; its spines drop off when it dies
4 (c) The cockle
5 (b) They are blue with brown markings
6 (a) 4.8 metres
7 (a) A barnacle
8 Although it looks like a limpet, a barnacle is a crustacean; its shell is made up of a number of plates
9 (c) 800
10 (b) Red
11 10
12 (a) The spiny starfish, which has been found measuring 35 centimetres. The common starfish can measure anything from 5 centimetres to 25 centimetres
13 Animals
14 (c) The common lobster. It is usually 8–20 centimetres long and weighs 1–1.5 kilograms
15 (c) In sand or sandy mud
16 By counting the rings on its shell
17 Yes
18 (c) On stalks
19 Their feelers
20 (b) It is a very beautiful sponge found in the Philippines
21 (b) Their arms have suckers on them so they can pull the shell open
22 (b) A cuttle fish. It has a siphon below its arms; if alarmed, it forces water out of this and shoots backwards
23 (c) Tiny animals. They secrete the coral which forms an external skeleton
24 (b) In the empty shell of a winkle or whelk
25 (a) Mussels
26 True. The body is shaped like an umbrella and, by opening and closing it, the jellyfish moves along

The Record Breakers (pp. 52–5)

1 The blue whale
2 The cheetah, which can reach a speed of about 96 kilometres per hour over level ground
3 (b) The Alaskan moose. The red deer is the largest in Britain
4 The ostrich
5 (c) The head and body of a goliath frog from West Africa measured 81.5 centimetres
6 (b) 70 years
7 (b) 5 metres
8 (b) Over 22,000
9 The roe deer
10 (b) The swallowtail
11 The giraffe. The bulls (males) are about 5.5 metres high
12 (b) The weasel. The snipe is a bird and rabbits eat greenstuff
13 (a) 2 grams
14 The coypu. It lives in East Anglia and is a rat-like animal as big as a cocker spaniel

Dinosaurs and Other Prehistoric Animals (pp. 56–62)

1 (a) Fish. They had lungs and strong fins which gradually changed to legs, and they became amphibians
2 (b) Dinosaurs
3 (a) The size of a hen's egg. It had another nerve-centre which controlled its hind legs and tail
4 Terrible lizard
5 Both. There were two kinds of dinosaur: meat-eaters and plant-eaters
6 Triceratops
7 Thunder lizard
8 (a) 35 tonnes
9 (c) Stegosaurus. This 'armour' helped protect it from meat-eating dinosaurs
10 (b) As long as three buses – about 27 metres
11 Tyrannosaurus
12 (b) Roof lizard. The plates along its back are like roof tiles
13 (b) 60 million years ago
14 (b) It is thought that when the climate got colder they were too big to keep warm or find shelter
15 (c) Traces of an organism preserved in rock

16 (b) Stone. Layers of mud and sand that covered the organism turn to rock; then the organism is gradually replaced by minerals which form an exact stone copy of it

17 Yes. Fossils of a whole nest of eggs of protoceratops have been found in the Gobi Desert

18 (c) To keep warm. They could stand sideways and warm up the blood in the 'sail' or face the sun to cool down

19 (b) 40 million years ago

20 (c) A kind of elephant. It developed a thick layer of fat under its skin and long woolly hair to keep warm in the Ice Age

21 (b) Tar. Rainwater lay on the surface of these pools, so animals like elephants went to drink, not realizing that the tar was there. Other animals like sabre-toothed cats who went to eat the struggling elephants sometimes fell into the tar, too

22 A mammal's. Reptiles have only one sort of tooth – sharp and pointed

23 (b) Frozen in ice. If they were dug out, they began to rot

24 (b) Australia

25 (a) A palaeontologist. An ornithologist studies birds and a meteorologist studies the weather

Habitats (pp. 63–7)

1 No. Many spend all their lives wandering, for example the kangaroo

2 Africa

3 Yes – even some toads which need water for their eggs to develop

4 (c) On the rock of Gibraltar

5 (b) The elephant – the others stay in the rain forest

6 (b) Canada

7 (c) By sleeping in the day and being active at night

8 (a) Australia

9 (a) In a swamp

10 (b) The pine marten

11 (b) Reptiles. They can wait for water, as they are able to slow down their metabolism

12 (c) New Guinea. There are forty species, some with exotic names like the lesser superb bird of paradise!

13 (c) The yak. This is the wild ox of Tibet and Szechwan and lives as high up as 6,000 metres

14 (b) To hunt for shrimps and crabs

15 (b) They are covered in fur – even the soles

16 (a) China

17 (b) 10 centimetres
18 The Great Barrier Reef, off the north-east coast of Australia
19 (b) New Zealand
20 (c) Madagascar. There are many species of animal found only on this island
21 South; only the Galapagos penguin, which lives wild on these islands on the Equator, might wander north
22 (c) The wind – which carries pollen and seeds up from the plains
23 (a) Herrings. Tench and piranhas are freshwater fish

Primates (pp. 68–71)

1 The gorilla
2 The big toes can work opposite the others like a thumb to help them climb
3 Monkeys have tails; some can use their tails like an extra leg to hold on to branches
4 (a) Gibbons
5 Gorillas walk on all fours. Their weight is taken by pads on their knuckles
6 (a) Proboscis monkeys, which live in the trees and also swim among the roots
7 (b) In the rain forest, which is very dense
8 (c) 10 metres
9 (b) A mandrill
10 The baboon
11 (a) Orang-utans
12 (c) The marmoset
13 (b) The siamang, which is a species of gibbon
14 (b) Chimpanzees move around so much that they build a nest every day at dusk. It is about 15 metres above ground, and made of branches pulled together with leaves on top

Mammals (pp. 72–8)

1 (b) About 200 million years ago
2 (c) The Etruscan shrew
3 Cats
4 A brush
5 (b) 7 grams
6 (b) Very fine hair which is called velvet
7 Yes. As they swim, they close their nostrils to shut out the water

8 A platypus

9 (c) Australia

10 African elephants are larger and they have bigger ears

11 (b) The puma

12 The beaver, which is clever enough to fell them towards or into the river, ready to make a dam

13 (c) A deer

14 (b) Scavengers are animals like hyaenas and vultures that eat the remains of other animals' meals

15 The elephant. The knee-joint of the back legs of other four-legged animals is too high up

16 (b) To protect their feet from hot sand

17 Bats

18 (a) 1½ years

19 (b) 30 minutes

20 (b) Fat. Camels can't store water but they use what is in their body very economically

21 (c) 115 litres

22 The Bactrian camel

23 (c) So that they stay sharp – they can also move about more easily

24 (a) Tree trunks

25 Yes

26 Red

27 (a) Leopards. They are lighter and have longer tails to help them balance

28 At night

29 14

30 The buffalo

31 Elephants. They like to cool themselves by spraying water over their bodies with their trunks

32 (b) A one-humped Arabian camel. These camels are used for riding

33 Black rats live at the top of buildings; brown rats live in cellars, stables and sewers

Birds (pp. 79–87)

1 (c) Reptiles. The earliest known bird, Archaeopteryx (illustrated on page 79), still had claws on its wings where its ancestors' 'hands' were.

2 (b) 8,580

3 No. Ostriches, kiwis and some others can't

4 Striped

5 The pelican

6 (a) The blackbird

7 (b) The bee hummingbird

8 (c) Seed-eating birds have stout beaks; insect-eating birds have thin and pointed beaks, and predators (meat-eating) have hooked beaks

9 (c) So the fish's scales don't stick in their throat

10 The great black-backed gull

11 The golden eagle

12 (c) About 25,000. In comparison, a thrush has about 2,000

13 The ostrich

14 (a) The dipper. It can walk upstream with its head down, searching for food; the force of a fast current on its back holds it on the river bed

15 (b) In a hole in a giant cactus in the desert

16 Ravens

17 (c) To catch food; it can filter food from the water with its beak

18 Falcons usually do, while hawks and eagles have large, rounded wings

19 (b) In the Arctic

20 (c) Green

21 (c) Hummingbirds

22 (c) In a hole in a tree trunk

23 (a) 13 months

24 (a) A shrike, also nicknamed 'butcher-bird'

25 (c) The wandering albatross, which averages just over 3 metres. The Andean condor has the largest wings

26 (b) The jay

27 (c) So they don't get messy pulling meat out of carcasses

28 There are lots to choose from: long-tailed tit, blue tit, coal-tit, great tit, marsh tit, crested tit

29 (b) By wedging it in the bark of a tree

30 (c) 2 months. He can shuffle about, but only very slowly

31 (c) Skuas

32 (a) A kiwi

33 (c) To catch fish just below the surface

34 (a) An avocet has the most upturned bill of any bird

35 (c) On the marshes

36 (b) By scraping with a cactus spine

37 None of them can fly

38 (a) Because it sings in all weathers

39 (a) Gulls. They gather in large flocks on the grassy areas. If they fly into an engine or propeller, they can cause a lot of damage

Markings and Camouflage (pp. 88–91)

1 Feathers
2 A toucan
3 (b) The proboscis monkey
4 (b) The spider crab
5 Every year
6 An amphibian
7 A stoat
8 (b) The sloth. Water and other debris can then fall out of its coat when it is hanging upside down
9 No. The lobster has to shed it and grow another one as it increases in size
10 (c) By the pattern of stripes on their bottoms
11 (b) The walrus. It uses its tusks as ice-picks, as well as for fighting and searching for food
12 A dolphin
13 Yes. You can see the fourth tooth on each side of a crocodile's lower jaw
14 (a) The fiddler crab

Reptiles (pp. 92–5)

1 It is forked at the end
2 (a) To get cool. Crocodiles can't sweat, so they open their mouths to allow moisture to evaporate and this cools them
3 No. It is a limbless lizard
4 (a) The estuarine crocodile; also called the saltwater crocodile. The longest recorded was 8.63 metres long
5 No. A poisonous snake has hollow teeth called poison fangs
6 (b) Lizards
7 It has dry segments of old, shed skins at the end of its tail which rattle when shaken
8 (b) To help identify smells
9 (b) The boa constrictor
10 Lungs
11 (b) The komodo dragon. They grow to over 3 metres long, and sometimes eat people
12 (c) 12
13 (c) They spend the night hunting in the water, out of the cold night air
14 The sidewinder; it lives in the deserts of the south-west United States

15 (a) Tortoises

16 To help them stay under water more easily

17 (a) The reticulated python. It can grow up to 10 metres in length

18 (b) The tiger snake of South Australia

Amphibians (pp. 96–8)

1 Frogs have soft, moist, smooth skin; toads have tough, dry skin

2 The left one

3 (a) They are black, but they have a red, yellow or orange belly, so they lie on their backs to show predators that they have poison in their skin

4 (a) A kind of salamander

5 (b) After rain

6 (b) With suckers which most tree frogs have on each toe

7 (b) The European spade-foot

8 (c) Some can grow to over 23 centimetres

9 (c) Termites

Insects (pp. 99–101)

1 Antennae

2 (c) 6

3 A ladybird

4 No. Damselflies, which are very similar, do

5 Moulting

6 (a) 5 or 6 times

7 Drones

8 (c) They roll them in a ball of dung which they then bury. The larvae can feed on the dung, and the beetles coincidentally fertilize the ground

9 The crane-fly

10 (c) The stag beetle. It can measure 6.5 centimetres

11 (c) The death-watch beetle. The tiger beetle eats insects and the colorado beetle eats plants

12 The bee

13 (c) Malaria

14 (b) To find out if they are from the same nest

15 (a) Termites

Spiders (pp. 102–104)

1 No, it is an arachnid. However, both insects and arachnids belong to the arthropod section of the animal kingdom.
2 (b) The raft spider. The female raft spider can have a body measuring 2 centimetres
3 (b) 8, in two rows of four
4 (b) Less than 170 grams – about the same weight as this book!
5 (c) Over 600
6 (c) By throwing a sticky blob on a line at the moth
7 (c) She eats the male
8 (b) Because they think they have caught a meal. Their legs are very sensitive to vibrations
9 (b) Up the bath waste-pipe
10 (b) The black widow
11 No
12 (b) It is caught by a safety rope. Jumping spiders trail a thread after them which catches them if they fall

Butterflies and Moths (pp. 105–109)

1 (a) A moth
  (b) A butterfly
2 Egg, caterpillar, chrysalis
3 (b) Comma
4 (c) Cabbage
5 Moths – approximately 2,000 species to 70 species of butterfly
6 (a) Fritillary
7 The caterpillar of the garden tiger-moth, which is very hairy
8 (a) It should be orange tip
9 The emperor moth caterpillar
10 (a) Hawk-moths
11 Nectar
12 The sun
13 The elephant hawk-moth
14 (b) A moth
15 (b) On nettles
16 (b) Peacock
17 (c) By encouraging red ants to live there – they eat the caterpillars
18 (b) Fritillary butterflies
19 (c) 5 miles
20 (c) Mulberry leaves

21 (c) Around the tops of forest oak trees

22 (b) 1979

Fish (pp. 110–16)

1 (b) Smelling the water

2 (c) Around coral reefs

3 (c) Perch; it is a freshwater fish, which means that it lives in rivers, lakes or ponds rather than the sea

4 A seahorse

5 The dorsal fins keep the fish balanced and upright, the tail fin pushes it forward and the pectoral fins help it to go up and down

6 (c) The whale shark, which can grow to 18 metres long

7 (b) The salmon

8 (b) The barracuda; the little cleaner fish cleans the barracuda's teeth and is unharmed by it

9 A freshwater lobster

10 (c) The weever. It half buries itself in sand with the poisonous spines on its dorsal fin sticking up. It is extremely painful if you tread on it

11 (c) The tarpon which can be 2.4 metres long. (Big fish don't always have big scales)

12 (a) Sweetlips (b) Snapper (c) Clown-fish

13 A shoal

14 (b) In South American rivers, especially the Amazon

15 (b) On the seabed

16 (c) Fruit that falls from the trees into the river

17 (c) The pike

18 (b) They have antifreeze in their blood

19 No. Their eyes are always open

20 A cuttlefish. You sometimes find the oval white layered shell of a cuttlefish on the beach. It is called a cuttlebone

21 (a) They use the sun and stars to cross the ocean. But they can smell their home river as soon as they are near it

22 Spawn

23 (b) The flounder

24 (a) The manta ray, which can be 6.7 metres wide

25 In warm water; attacks in cold water are almost unknown

26 (c) Parrot-fish

27 (b) The coelacanth – pronounced seal-oh-kanth

28 (c) The mudskipper. It lives in mangrove swamps and uses its pectoral fins to crawl along and climb

29 (a) The carp

30 (a) The lamprey

31 A hammerhead shark

32 (c) 5 years. It makes a cocoon in the mud and waits

33 (b) A line of nerve-endings along the side of all bony fish like trout and sardines

34 (a) Pollack. The crabs and fish which shelter in the growth around the wreck provide a good supply of food. There are also plenty of holes to hide in!

Nocturnal Animals (pp. 117–20)

1 It has huge eyes

2 The hedgehog

3 (c) The nightingale

4 No. Their 'ears' are long head-feathers and have no connection with hearing

5 Hanging upside-down

6 (b) The slug

7 By sight. Smaller bats navigate by sound

8 (b) The ghost crab

9 (c) Its tongue. It has a sticky tongue about 30 centimetres long which it pokes into termites' nests

10 (b) Sleeping in deep burrows

11 (b) The pipistrelle

12 (b) The owl monkey

13 (c) The New Forest

14 (a) Over 200

15 (c) A badger

16 (b) They use the two big claws on their hind legs

Winter Changes (pp. 121–4)

1 Hibernation

2 Migration

3 (b) In the mud at the bottom of a pond

4 The monarch. It is the only butterfly in the world that regularly migrates north and south as birds do

5 (c) Not at all. When they go to sleep, their heart rate drops and everything slows down so they can manage without food

6 (a) The Arctic tern. It flies 11,000 miles from North America or Greenland to South America

7 No; for instance, storks leave Central Europe and take two different routes to the same place in Africa while others go further south in Africa, or to Arabia

8 (c) On the seabed

9 (b) Yellow

10 (b) In polar waters, feeding. As whales do not naturally cross the Equator, there are two separate populations of them. They don't meet because the seasons are opposite in the southern and northern hemispheres, so both lots go south at the same time

11 (b) Africa

12 (a) Fat. They store it up during the summer

13 (b) They grow a new, white coat. Stoats are called ermine when they look like this

14 (c) Antarctica

Hunting (pp. 125–7)

1 (b) The archer-fish

2 At night

3 (c) A polar bear. A killer whale would attack them in the water

4 (b) By digging a sandpit for them to fall into

5 (b) A tarantula, which is also called a bird-eating spider

6 Females. Males guard the territory

7 (b) Under a pile of leaves. Leopards can carry their prey up trees

8 An octopus

9 (a) Moose and caribou

10 (a) The reddish egret

11 (a) They can sense the heat of warm-blooded creatures by means of a heat-sensitive pit situated between eye and nostril

12 (c) Stooping

Eating Habits (pp. 128–32)

1 (b) Eucalyptus leaves

2 A meat-eating animal, such as a lion

3 No. Bears eat both animal and plant food

4 (a) Monkeys

5 Whole

6 No. The caterpillars which hatch from their eggs do. The moths do not feed

7 (b) The gizzard

8 (c) Berries. They also eat grasses and insects

9 To keep their coats waterproof

10 The common vampire

11 (c) Grass

12 (a) The North American porcupine

13 True. Their 'cows' are plant lice which give off honeydew when stroked by the ants

14 (b) The chipmunk

15 (b) Squid. It has been estimated that over 100 million tonnes of squid are eaten by sperm whales every year!

16 Animals like deer, giraffes, goats and cows swallow food quickly and then return it to the mouth to be re-chewed. This process is called 'chewing the cud'

17 (c) 4 – like a cow's

18 No. Males live on plant juices

19 The black rhinoceros eats leaves, and the white eats grass

20 (c) Pine-cones

21 (b) The robber crab which lives on coral islands

22 (c) A stone

23 (b) The kea

24 (c) 438 in eight years

Defence (pp. 133–6)

1 (c) Because they can see predators in time to avoid them

2 (b) By inflating themselves so they look frightening and too large to be gobbled up

3 (b) Stink glands

4 The gorilla

5 (b) Among clumps of cactus

6 (a) By pretending to be dead. Grass snakes have no sting or poison fangs

7 It squirts out dark-brown ink

8 (c) By running away. It is a deer-like animal that can move very fast

9 (c) The armadillo. It is covered with hard, bony plates

10 (c) They leave their attacker holding a wriggling tail, giving themselves time to run off

11 (c) By squirting venom into the eyes of its enemy. It can do this from a distance of 4 metres

12 (b) With a nozzle on their heads that shoots out a sticky repellent

Animals in Danger (pp. 137–41)

1 (a) Over 1,000
2 It is the protection of animals, their habitats and their food
3 (b) Orang-utans
4 (c) Hats
5 (b) The wolf
6 Whales
7 (a) The blue whale
8 (b) The Nile crocodile
9 (a) The savannah or grassland areas of Africa
10 The American bison, which became extinct in the wild in 1930 but still exists in reserves
11 (b) Central Wales
12 The pine marten
13 (c) Reindeer
14 (a) When explorers went to Mauritius, the dodos were caught and killed by the pigs they took with them – they couldn't escape by flying away
15 (c) Every minute
16 (b) Russia
17 (c) Discarded fishing tackle
18 (b) They carry disease. This prevents people and cattle from settling in certain areas and thus preserves them in their natural state
19 (b) Books describing animals and plants in danger of extinction

Animals and their Uses (pp. 142–51)

1 (c) 35 pints (20 litres)
2 (c) Pigs
3 Sheep – their wool can be spun into lengths and used for knitting
4 (b) 6
5 (b) India
6 The meat from sheep that are more than a year old
7 (c) Mushrooms
8 (c) Pigs
9 (c) The eider duck. It lines its nest with its own feathers
10 Yes – from the nests of cave swiftlets of South-east Asia and Indonesia
11 (c) The camel
12 (c) About 2 million
13 (b) Meat from deer

14 (b) Dagger handles. In East Asia they are used for carving and in medicine

15 (b) The jungle fowl, a common pheasant of South-east Asia

16 (c) The adhesive with which barnacles cling to a boat could be adapted into a cement for tooth fillings

17 (a) Poison from the skin of tree frogs. They heat the frogs over a fire to make them sweat out the poison

18 (b) India. The single-celled animals that cause the disease only develop in the bodies of the mosquitoes when the temperature is hotter than 24°C

19 (a) The giant rat, although the other two are also eaten

20 (b) Malaysia

21 (a) Termites

22 (a) These birds have highly developed hearts and excellent circulation to be able to fly so far, so they are helpful for the study of diseases of the heart and circulatory system

23 (c) The bison. The new animal can also reach a weight of 450 kilograms in half the time

24 (a) The wild toad; 100,000 toad legs a year can be sold to be eaten in Chile and abroad

25 (c) Shrimps. They are probably the world's most valuable wild animal because so many are sold

26 (a) The rhesus monkey. Primates are most helpful because of their close relationship to human beings

27 (a) South America, followed by Asia

28 (b) Elephants – their tusks are ivory

29 (b) Raw potato and lettuce

30 (c) The woodpecker. High-speed films have shown that the woodpecker hammers against a tree trunk at a speed of over 300 kilometres per hour without injuring itself

31 (a) The bee

32 (a) Bali, one of the islands of Indonesia

33 (c) Fish called tilapias. In large enough numbers, they can clear the weed

34 (c) The skeletons of crabs, shrimps and lobsters

35 (c) 400 gallons (1820 litres)

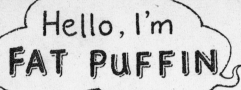